of

Happiness

A GUIDEBOOK
FOR LIVING

His Holiness the Dalai Lama
and Howard C. Cutler, M.D.

HODDER

MOBIUS

Hodder & Stoughton

Copyright © 2001 by HH Dalai Lama and Howard C. Cutler, M.D.

First published in Australia and New Zealand in 2001
by Hodder Headline Australia Pty Limited
First published in Great Britain in 2002 by Hodder and Stoughton
A division of Hodder Headline

5

A CIP catalogue record for this title is available from the British Library

Printed and bound in Great Britain by
Clays Ltd, St Ives plc

Hodder and Stoughton
A division of Hodder Headline
338 Euston Road
London NW1 3BH

Contents

Foreword

The Essence of Happiness has been extracted from *The Art of Happiness: A Handbook for Living*, a book based on extensive conversations between His Holiness the Dalai Lama and Dr Howard C. Cutler, a Western psychiatrist. Dr Cutler's aim was to collaborate on a project that would present the Dalai Lama's views on leading a happier life, augmented by observations and commentary from his own Western perspective.

Dr Cutler received his medical degree from the University of Arizona College of Medicine. He completed specialty training in psychiatry at the Good Samaritan Medical Centre in Phoenix, and is a diplomate of the American Board of Psychiatry and Neurology. Dr Cutler currently resides in Phoenix, where he has a private psychiatric practice.

His Holiness Tenzin Gyatso, the Fourteenth Dalai Lama, is the spiritual and temporal leader of the Tibetan people. In 1989 His Holiness was awarded the Nobel Peace Prize for his non-violent struggle for the liberation of Tibet. Since 1959 he has been living in exile in India. Tibet continues to be occupied by Communist China.

The High Office of Tibet
Dharamsala
India
February 2001

Preface

Howard C. Cutler MD met His Holiness the Dalai Lama in 1982, while visiting India on a research grant to study traditional Tibetan medicine. Impressed by the Dalai Lama's many remarkable qualities, particularly his serenity and sense of fulfilment, he began to wonder if he could elicit from the Dalai Lama a set of practices that could be used by non-Buddhists in the pursuit of a happier life. The extensive conversations that ensued, both in India and during the Dalai Lama's visit to Arizona in 1993, culminated in the bestselling *Art of Happiness*.

The Essence of Happiness presents a quintessential selection of the Dalai Lama's views on the nature of happiness and how it may be achieved, based on 2500 years of Buddhist thought and meditation, coupled with the observations and commentary of Howard C. Cutler from his perspective as a Western psychiatrist.

His Holiness the Dalai Lama believes that 'The very purpose of our life is happiness; the very motion of our life is towards happiness', and *The Essence of Happiness* presents this vision of happiness as an attainable objective—one that we can take positive steps towards achieving on a daily basis. As we begin to identify the factors that lead to a happier life, we will learn how the search for happiness offers benefits not only for the individual but also for the individual's family and for society at large as well. *The Essence of Happiness* shows us that with compassion, love and training of the mind, happiness is achievable for everyone.

PART I

The Purpose of Life

I believe that the very purpose of our life is to seek happiness. That is clear. Whether one believes in religion or not, whether one believes in this religion or that religion, we all are seeking something better in life. So, I think, the very motion of our life is towards happiness.

The purpose of our life is happiness. That simple statement can be used as a powerful tool in helping us navigate through life's daily problems. From that perspective, our task becomes one of discarding the things that lead to suffering and accumulating the things that lead to happiness. The method, the daily practice, involves gradually increasing our awareness and understanding of what truly leads to happiness and what doesn't.—H.C.

The purpose of our life needs to be positive. We weren't born with the purpose of causing trouble, harming others. For our life to be of value, I think we must develop basic good human qualities—warmth, kindness, compassion. Then our life becomes meaningful and more peaceful—happier.

The concept of achieving true happiness has, in the West, always seemed ill-defined, elusive, ungraspable. Even the word 'happy' is derived from the Icelandic word happ, *meaning luck or chance... The Dalai Lama's method for achieving happiness is based on the revolutionary idea that negative mental states are not an intrinsic part of our minds; they are transient obstacles that obstruct the expression of our underlying natural state of joy and happiness.*—H.C.

I always believe we are the same; we are all human beings. Of course, there may be differences in cultural background or way of life, there may be differences in our faith, or we may be of a different colour, but we are human beings, consisting of the human body and the human mind. Our physical structure is the same, and our mind and our emotional nature are also the same. Wherever I meet people, I always have the feeling that I am encountering another human being, just like myself. I find it is much easier to communicate with others on that level... If we can leave the differences aside, I think we can easily communicate, exchange ideas and share experiences.

Although it is possible to achieve happiness, happiness is not a simple thing. There are many levels. In Buddhism, for instance, there is a reference to the four factors of fulfilment, or happiness: wealth, worldly satisfaction, spirituality and enlightenment. Together they embrace the totality of an individual's quest for happiness.

'Is happiness a reasonable goal for most of us?' I asked the Dalai Lama. 'Is it really possible?' And he replied, 'Yes. I believe that happiness can be achieved through training the mind.'—H.C.

When I say 'training the mind,' in this context I'm not referring to 'mind' merely as one's cognitive ability or intellect. Rather, I'm using the term in the sense of the Tibetan word *Sem*, which has a much broader meaning, closer to 'psyche' or 'spirit'; it includes intellect and feeling, heart and mind. By bringing about a certain inner discipline, we can undergo a transformation of our attitude, our entire outlook and approach to living.

Survey after survey has shown that it is unhappy people who tend to be most self-focused and are often socially withdrawn, brooding, and even antagonistic. Happy people, in contrast, are generally found to be more sociable, flexible and creative, and are able to tolerate life's daily frustrations more easily than unhappy people. And, most important, they are found to be more loving and forgiving than unhappy people... Happiness is determined more by one's state of mind than by external events.—H.C.

When we speak of this inner discipline, it can of course involve many things, many methods. But generally speaking, one begins by identifying those factors which lead to happiness and those factors which lead to suffering. Having done this, one then sets about gradually eliminating those factors which lead to suffering and cultivating those which lead to happiness. That is the way.

Our feelings of contentment are strongly influenced by our tendency to compare… Constant comparison with those who are smarter, more beautiful or more successful than ourselves also tends to breed envy, frustration and unhappiness. But we can use this same principle in a positive way; we can increase our feeling of life satisfaction by comparing ourselves to those who are less fortunate than us and by reflecting on all the things we have.—H.C.

If we utilise our favourable circumstances, such as our good health or wealth, in positive ways, in helping others, they can be contributory factors in achieving a happier life. And of course we enjoy these things—our material facilities, success and so on. But without the right mental attitude, without attention to the mental factor, these things have very little impact on our long-term feelings of happiness. For example, if you harbour hateful thoughts or intense anger somewhere deep down within yourself, then it ruins your health; thus it destroys one of the factors.

The greater the level of calmness of our mind, the greater our peace of mind, the greater our ability to enjoy a happy and joyful life.

When we speak of a calm state of mind or peace of mind, we shouldn't confuse that with a totally insensitive, apathetic state of mind. Having a calm or peaceful state of mind doesn't mean being totally spaced out or completely empty. Peace of mind or a calm state of mind is rooted in affection and compassion. There is a very high level of sensitivity and feeling there.

As long as there is a lack of the inner discipline that brings calmness of mind, no matter what external facilities or conditions you have, they will never give you the feeling of joy and happiness that you are seeking. On the other hand, if you possess this inner quality, a calmness of mind, a degree of stability within, then even if you lack various external facilities that you would normally consider necessary for happiness, it is still possible to live a happy and joyful life.

One interesting thing about greed is that although the underlying motive is to seek satisfaction, the irony is that even after obtaining the object of your desire, you are still not satisfied. The true antidote of greed is contentment. If you have a strong sense of contentment, it doesn't matter whether you obtain the object or not; either way, you are still content.

The demarcation between a positive and a negative desire or action is not whether it gives you an immediate feeling of satisfaction but whether it ultimately results in positive or negative consequences.

Now sometimes people confuse happiness with pleasure... from my point of view, the highest happiness is when one reaches the stage of Liberation, at which there is no more suffering. That's genuine, lasting happiness. True happiness relates more to the mind and heart. Happiness that depends mainly on physical pleasure is unstable; one day it's there, the next day it may not be.

*Framing any decision we face by asking
ourselves, 'Will it bring me happiness?' That
simple question can be a powerful tool in
helping us skilfully conduct all areas of our
lives, not just in the decision whether to
indulge in drugs or that third piece of
banana cream pie. It puts a new slant on
things. Approaching our daily decisions and
choices with this question in mind shifts the
focus from what we are denying ourselves to
what we are seeking—ultimate happiness.*
—H.C.

B ut there is another source of worth and dignity from which you can relate to fellow human beings. You can relate to them because you are still a human being, within the human community. You share that bond. And that human bond is enough to give rise to a sense of worth and dignity. That bond can become a source of consolation in the event that you lose everything else.

We don't need more money, we don't need greater success or fame, we don't need the perfect body or even the perfect mate—right now, at this very moment, we have a mind, which is all the basic equipment we need to achieve complete happiness.—H.C.

The first step in seeking happiness is learning. We first have to learn how negative emotions and behaviours are harmful to us and how positive emotions are helpful. And we must realise how these negative emotions are not only very bad and harmful to one personally but harmful to society and the future of the whole world as well.

If you desire happiness, you should seek the causes that give rise to it, and if you don't desire suffering, then what you should do is to ensure that the causes and conditions that would give rise to it no longer arise.

Proper utilisation of time is so important. While we have this body, and especially this amazing human brain, I think every minute is something precious. Our day-to-day existence is very much alive with hope, although there is no guarantee of our future. There is no guarantee that tomorrow at this time we will be here. But still we are working for that purely on the basis of hope. So, we need to make the best use of our time. I believe that the proper utilisation of time is this: if you can, serve other people, other sentient beings. If not, at least refrain from harming them. I think that is the whole basis of my philosophy.

Achieving genuine happiness may require bringing about a transformation in your outlook, your way of thinking, and this is not a simple matter.

You shouldn't have the notion...that there is just one key, a secret, and if you can get that right, then everything will be okay. It is similar to taking proper care of the physical body; you need a variety of vitamins and nutrients, not just one or two. In the same way, in order to achieve happiness you need a variety of approaches and methods to deal with and overcome the varied and complex negative mental states.

*C*hange takes time.

And in the same way, transforming your mind takes time. There are a lot of negative mental traits, so you need to address and counteract each one of these. That isn't easy. It requires the repeated application of various techniques and taking the time to familiarise yourself with the practices. It's a process of learning.

*E*veryday, as soon as you get up, you can develop a sincere positive motivation, thinking, 'I will utilise this day in a more positive way. I should not waste this very day.' And then, at night before bed, check what you've done, asking yourself, 'Did I utilise this day as I planned?

At the beginning, the implementation of the positive practices is very small, so the negative influences are still very powerful. However, eventually, as you gradually build up the positive practices, the negative behaviours are automatically diminished... Through repeated practice of these methods we can get to the point where some disturbance may occur but the negative effects on our mind remain on the surface, like the waves that may ripple on the surface of an ocean but don't have much effect deep down.

No matter what activity or practice we are pursuing, there isn't anything that isn't made easier through constant familiarity and training. Through training, we can change; we can transform ourselves.

Whether our action is wholesome
or unwholesome depends on
whether that action or deed arises from a
disciplined or undisciplined state of
mind. It is felt that a disciplined mind
leads to happiness and an undisciplined
mind leads to suffering, and in fact it is
said that bringing about discipline within
one's mind is the essence of the Buddha's
teaching.

PART II

Human Warmth and Compassion

Now, we are made to seek happiness. And it is clear that feelings of love, affection, closeness and compassion bring happiness. I believe that every one of us has the basis to be happy, to access the warm and compassionate states of mind that bring happiness. In fact, it is one of my fundamental beliefs that not only do we inherently possess the potential for compassion but I believe that the basic or underlying nature of human beings is gentleness.

*O*ur physical structure seems to be more suited to feelings of love and compassion. We can see how a calm, affectionate, wholesome state of mind has beneficial effects on our health and physical wellbeing. Conversely, feelings of frustration, fear, agitation and anger can be destructive to our health.

When human intelligence and human goodness or affection are used together, all human actions become constructive. When we combine a warm heart with knowledge and education, we can learn to respect others' views and others' rights. This becomes the basis of a spirit of reconciliation that can be used to overcome aggression and resolve our conflict. So, no matter how much violence or how many bad things we have to go through, I believe that the ultimate solution to our conflicts, both internal and external, lies in returning to our basic or underlying human nature, which is gentle and compassionate.

I look at any human being from a more positive angle; I try to look for their positive aspects. This attitude immediately creates a feeling of affinity, a kind of connectedness.

I would regard a compassionate, warm, kindhearted person as healthy. If you maintain a feeling of compassion, loving kindness, then something automatically opens your inner door. Through that, you can communicate much more easily with other people. And that feeling of warmth creates a kind of openness. You'll find that all human beings are just like you, so you'll be able to relate to them more easily.

My basic belief is that you first need to realise the usefulness of compassion.

I think that in many cases people tend to expect the other person to respond to them in a positive way first, rather than taking the initiative themselves to create that possibility. I feel that's wrong; it leads to problems and can act as a barrier that just serves to promote a feeling of isolation from others. So, if you wish to overcome that feeling of isolation and loneliness, I think that your underlying attitude makes a tremendous difference. And approaching others with the thought of compassion in your mind is the best way to do this.

Within all beings there is the seed of perfection. However, compassion is required in order to activate that seed which is inherent in our hearts and minds.

Whenever I meet people I always approach them from the standpoint of the most basic things we have in common. We each have a physical structure, a mind, emotions. We are all born in the same way, and we all die. All of us want happiness and do not want to suffer. Looking at others from this standpoint rather than emphasising secondary differences, such as the fact that I am Tibetan, or a different colour, religion or cultural background, allows me to have a feeling that I'm meeting someone just the same as me. I find that relating to others on that level makes it much easier to exchange and communicate with one another.

I think that empathy is important not only as a means of enhancing compassion, but I think that generally speaking, when dealing with others on any level, if you're having some difficulties, it's extremely helpful to be able to try to put yourself in the other person's place and see how you would react to the situation.

On a personal level, being open and sharing things can be very useful. Because of this nature I can make friends more easily, and it's not just a matter of knowing people and having a superficial exchange but of really sharing my deepest problems and suffering. And it's the same thing when I hear good news; I immediately share it with others. So, I feel a sense of intimacy and connection with my friends.

I think that if one is seeking to build a truly satisfying relationship, the best way of bringing this about is to get to know the deeper nature of the person and relate to her or him on that level, instead of merely on the basis of superficial characteristics. And in this type of relationship there is a role for genuine compassion.

I think that, leaving aside how the endless pursuit of romantic love may affect our deeper spiritual growth, even from the perspective of a conventional way of life, the idealisation of this romantic love can be seen as an extreme. Unlike those relationships based on caring and genuine affection, this is another matter... It's something that is based on fantasy, unattainable, and therefore may be a source of frustration. So, on that basis it cannot be seen as a positive thing.

The factor that sustains a genuine friendship is a feeling of affection.

Compassion can be roughly defined in terms of a state of mind that is non-violent, non-harming and non-aggressive. It is a mental attitude based on the wish for others to be free of their suffering and is associated with a sense of commitment, responsibility and respect towards the other.

think that there is often a danger of confusing compassion with attachment. So when we discuss compassion, we must first make a distinction between two types of love or compassion. One kind of compassion is tinged with attachment—the feeling of controlling someone, or loving someone so that person will love you back. This ordinary type of love or compassion is quite partial and biased. And a relationship based on that alone is unstable. But there is a second type of compassion that is free from such attachment. That is genuine compassion. That kind of compassion isn't so much based on the fact that this person or that person is dear to me. Rather, genuine compassion is based on the rationale that all human beings have an innate desire to be happy and overcome suffering, just like myself. And, just like myself, they have the natural right to fulfil this fundamental aspiration.

In developing compassion, perhaps one could begin with the wish that oneself be free of suffering, and then take that natural feeling towards oneself and cultivate it, enhance it and extend it out to include and embrace others.

In one sense one could define compassion as the feeling of unbearableness at the sight of other people's suffering, other sentient beings' suffering. And in order to generate that feeling one must first have an appreciation of the seriousness or intensity of another's suffering. So, I think that the more fully one understands suffering, and the various kinds of suffering that we are subject to, the deeper will be one's level of compassion.

In generating compassion, when you are taking on another's suffering, you may also initially experience a certain degree of discomfort, a sense of uncomfortableness or unbearableness. But in the case of compassion, the feeling is much different; underlying the uncomfortable feeling is a very high level of alertness and determination because you are voluntarily and deliberately accepting another's suffering for a higher purpose. There is a feeling of connectedness and commitment, a willingness to reach out to others, a feeling of freshness rather than dullness.

In generating compassion, you start by recognising that you do not want suffering and that you have a right to have happiness. This can be verified or validated by your own experience. You then recognise that other people, just like yourself, also do not want to suffer and that they have a right to have happiness. So this becomes the basis of your beginning to generate compassion.

PART III

Transforming
Suffering

Trying to avoid our problems or simply not thinking about them may provide temporary relief, but I think that there is a better approach. If you directly confront your suffering, you will be in a better position to appreciate the depth and nature of the problem. If you are in a battle, as long as you remain ignorant of the status and combat capability of your enemy, you will be totally unprepared and paralysed by fear. But if you know the fighting capability of your opponents, what sort of weapons they have and so on, then you're in a much better position when you engage in the war.

*O*ur attitude towards suffering becomes very important because it can affect how we cope with suffering when it arises. Now, our usual attitude consists of an intense aversion and intolerance of our pain and suffering. However, if we can transform our attitude towards suffering, adopt an attitude that allows us greater tolerance of it, then this can do much to help counteract feelings of mental unhappiness, dissatisfaction and discontent.

The point that has to be borne in mind is that the reason why reflection on suffering is so important is because there is a possibility of a way out; there is an alternative. There is a possibility of freedom from suffering.

Initially, of course, feelings of grief and anxiety are a natural human response to a loss. But if you allow these feelings of loss and worry to persist, there's a danger; if these feelings are left unchecked, they can lead to a kind of self-absorption.

If you find yourself worrying too much, it may help to think of the other people who have similar or even worse tragedies. Once you realise that, then you no longer feel isolated, as if you have been single-pointedly picked out. That can offer you some kind of condolence.

As long as we view suffering as an unnatural state, an abnormal condition that we fear, avoid and reject, we will never uproot the causes of suffering and begin to live a happier life.—H.C.

Although you may not always be able to avoid difficult situations, you can modify the extent to which you suffer by how you choose to respond to the situation.

In our daily life, problems invariably arise. But problems themselves do not automatically cause suffering. If we can directly address our problem and focus our energies on finding a solution, for instance, the problem can be transformed into a challenge.—H.C.

If we carefully examine any given situation in a very unbiased and honest way, we will realise that to a large extent we are also responsible for the unfolding of events.

It seems that whenever there are intense emotions involved, there tends to be a disparity between how things appear and how they really are.

Whether we are successful or not, even the honest attempt to search for our own contribution to a problem allows a certain shift of focus that helps to break through the narrow patterns of thinking that lead to the destructive feeling of unfairness that is the source of so much discontent in ourselves and in the world.

The beginning of being released from suffering is to investigate one of the primary causes: resistance to change.—H.C.

It's extremely important to investigate the causes or origins of suffering, how it arises. One must begin that process by appreciating the impermanent, transient nature of our existence. All things, events and phenomena are dynamic, changing every moment; nothing remains static.

The act of acceptance, of acknowledging that change is a natural part of our interactions with others, can play a vital role in our relationships. We may discover that it is at the very time when we may feel most disappointed, as if something has gone out of the relationship, that a profound transformation can occur.—H.C.

The ability to look at events from different perspectives can be very helpful. Then, practising this, one can use certain experiences, certain tragedies to develop a calmness of mind. One must realise that every phenomenon, every event, has different aspects. Everything is of a relative nature.

Hatred can be the greatest stumbling block to the development of compassion and happiness. If you can learn to develop patience and tolerance towards your enemies, then everything else becomes much easier—your compassion towards all others begins to flow naturally.

In fact, the enemy is the necessary condition for practising patience. Without an enemy's action, there is no possibility for patience or tolerance to arise. Our friends do not ordinarily test us and provide the opportunity to cultivate patience; only our enemies do this. So, from this standpoint we can consider our enemy as a great teacher, and revere him or her for giving us this precious opportunity to practise patience.

Generally speaking, once you're already in a difficult situation, it isn't possible to change your attitude simply by adopting a particular thought once or twice. Rather it's a process of learning, training and getting used to new viewpoints that enables you to deal with the difficulty.

The time and effort we spend searching for meaning in suffering will pay great rewards when bad things begin to strike. But in order to reap those rewards, we must begin our search for meaning when things are going well. A tree with strong roots can withstand the most violent storm, but the tree can't grow roots just as the storm appears on the horizon.—H.C.

A balanced and skilful approach to life, taking care to avoid extremes, becomes a very important factor in conducting one's everyday existence. It is important in all aspects of life.

Without cultivating a pliant mind, our out-look becomes brittle and our relationship to the world becomes characterised by fear. But by adopting a flexible, malleable approach to life, we can maintain our composure even in the most restless and turbulent conditions. It is through our efforts to achieve a flexible mind that we can nurture the resilience of the human spirit.—H.C.

Now there are many, many people in the world, but relatively few with whom we interact, and even fewer who cause us problems. So when you come across such a chance for practising patience and tolerance, you should treat it with gratitude. It is rare. Just as having unexpectedly found a treasure in your own house, you should be happy and grateful towards your enemy for providing that precious opportunity. Because if you are ever to be successful in your practice of patience and tolerance, which are critical factors in counteracting negative emotions, it is due to the combination of your own efforts and also the opportunity provided by your enemy.

Reflecting on suffering has tremendous importance because by realising the nature of suffering, you will develop greater resolve to put an end to the causes of suffering and the unwholesome deeds that lead to suffering. And it will increase your enthusiasm for engaging in the wholesome actions and deeds that lead to happiness and joy.

PART IV

Overcoming Obstacles

Whatever steps, however small, one can take towards learning to reduce the influence of the negative emotions can be very helpful. It can definitely help one live a happier and more satisfying life.

Learning and education are important because they help one develop conviction of the need to change, and help increase one's commitment. This conviction to change then develops into determination. Next, one transforms determination into action—the strong determination to change enables one to make a sustained effort to implement the actual changes. This final factor of effort is critical.

Now, no matter what behaviour you are seeking to change, no matter what particular goal or action you are directing your efforts towards, you need to start by developing a strong willingness or wish to do it. You need to generate great enthusiasm. And, here, a sense of urgency is a key factor. This sense of urgency is a powerful factor in helping you overcome problems.

In order to generate a sense of urgency to engage in spiritual practices, the practitioner is reminded of our impermanence, of death... That awareness of impermanence is encouraged, so that when it is coupled with our appreciation of the enormous potential of our human existence, it will give us a sense of urgency that we must use every precious moment.

By making a steady effort, I think we can overcome any form of negative conditioning and make positive changes in our lives. But you still need to realise that genuine change doesn't happen overnight.

*There is no getting around these essential
ingredients: determination, effort and time.
These are the real secrets to happiness.*
—H.C.

All 'deluded' states of mind, all afflictive emotions and thoughts, are essentially distorted, in that they are rooted in misperceiving the actual reality of the situation. No matter how powerful, deep down these negative emotions have no valid foundation. They are based on ignorance. On the other hand, all the positive emotions or states of mind, such as love, compassion, insight and so on, have a solid basis. When the mind is experiencing these positive states, there is no distortion.

The capacity to see things from different angles is quite selective; we can focus on a particular angle, a particular aspect of that phenomenon, and adopt a particular perspective. This capacity becomes very important when we seek to identify and eliminate certain negative aspects of ourselves or enhance positive traits. Because of this capacity to adopt a different perspective, we can isolate parts of ourselves that we seek to eliminate and do battle with them.

*O*ur positive states of mind can act as antidotes to our negative tendencies and delusory states of mind... As you enhance the capacity of these antidotal factors, the greater their force, the more you will be able to reduce the force of the mental and emotional afflictions, the more you will be able to reduce the influences and effects of these things.

The very fact that we can change our emotions and counteract negative thoughts by applying alternative ways of thinking lends support to the Dalai Lama's position that we can overcome our negative mental states through the application of the 'antidotes', or the corresponding positive mental states. And when this fact is combined with recent scientific evidence that we can change the structure and function of the brain by cultivating new thoughts, then the idea that we can achieve happiness through training of the mind seems a very real possibility.
—H.C.

Dealing with expectations is really a tricky issue. If you have excessive expectations without a proper foundation, then that usually leads to problems. On the other hand, without expectation and hope, without aspiration, there can be no progress. Some hope is essential. So finding the proper balance is not easy. One needs to judge each situation on the spot.

The essential nature of mind is pure. It is based on the belief that the underlying basic subtle consciousness is untainted by the negative emotions. Its nature is pure, a state which is referred to as the 'mind of Clear Light'. That basic nature of the mind is also called Buddha Nature. So, since the negative emotions are not an intrinsic part of this Buddha Nature, there is a possibility to eliminate them and purify the mind.

Hatred and anger are considered to be the greatest evils because they are the greatest obstacles to developing compassion and altruism, and they destroy one's virtue and calmness of mind.

We cannot overcome anger and hatred simply by suppressing them. We need to actively cultivate the antidotes to hatred: patience and tolerance… Someone who gains victory over hatred and anger through such an arduous process is a true hero.

*U*sually, we don't bother much about anger or hatred, so it just comes. But once we develop a cautious attitude towards these emotions, that reluctant attitude itself can act as a preventative measure against anger or hatred.

Feelings of anger and hatred arise from a mind that is troubled by dissatisfaction and discontent. So you can prepare ahead of time by constantly working towards building inner contentment and cultivating kindness and compassion. This brings about a certain calmness of mind that can help prevent anger from arising in the first place.

Since patience or tolerance comes from an ability to remain firm and steadfast and not be overwhelmed by the adverse situations or conditions that one faces, one should not see tolerance or patience as a sign of weakness or giving in, but rather as a sign of strength, coming from a deep ability to remain firm.

An end result or product of patience and tolerance is forgiveness. When you are truly patient and tolerant, then forgiveness comes naturally.

If the situation or problem is such that it can be remedied, then there is no need to worry about it. In other words, if there is a solution or a way out of the difficulty, then one needn't be overwhelmed by it. The appropriate action is to seek its solution. It is more sensible to spend the energy focusing on the solution rather than worrying about the problem. Alternatively, if there is no way out, no solution, no possibility of resolution, then there is also no point in being worried about it, because you can't do anything about it anyway.

In the Dalai Lama's system of training the mind and achieving happiness, the closer one gets to being motivated by altruism, the more fearless one becomes in the face of even extremely anxiety-provoking circumstances.—H.C.

Motivation is so important. In fact all human action can be seen in terms of movement, and the mover behind all actions is one's motivation. If you develop a pure and sincere motivation, if you are motivated by a wish to help on the basis of kindness, compassion and respect, then you can carry on any kind of work, in any field, and function more effectively with less fear or worry, not being afraid of what others think or whether you ultimately will be successful in reaching your goal.

J've found that sincere motivation acts as an antidote to reduce fear and anxiety.

One's sense of self, or 'ego,' is concerned only with the fulfilment of one's self-interest, one's selfish desires, with complete disregard for the wellbeing of others. The other type of ego or sense of self is based on a genuine concern for others and the desire to be of service. In order to fulfil that wish to be of service, one needs a strong sense of self, and a sense of self-confidence. This kind of self-confidence is the kind that leads to positive consequences.

The more honest you are, the more open, the less fear you will have, because there's no anxiety about being exposed or revealed to others. So, I think that the more honest you are, the more self-confident you will be.

PART V

On Living a
Spiritual Life

We often hear people say that all human beings are equal. By this we mean that everyone has the obvious desire of happiness. Everybody has the right to be a happy person. And everyone has the right to overcome suffering. So if someone is deriving happiness or benefit from a particular religious tradition, it becomes important to respect the rights of others; thus we must learn to respect all these major religious traditions. That is clear.

If we believe in any religion, that's good. But even without a religious belief, we can still manage. In some cases, we can manage even better. But that's our own individual right; if we wish to believe, good! If not, it's all right. But then there's another level of spirituality. That is what I call basic spirituality— basic human qualities of goodness, kindness, compassion, caring. Whether we are believers or non-believers, this kind of spirituality is essential. I personally consider this second level of spirituality to be more important than the first, because no matter how wonderful a particular religion may be, it will still only be accepted by a limited number of human beings, only a portion of humanity. But as long as we are human beings, as long as we are members of the human family, all of us need these basic spiritual values. Without these, human existence remains hard, very dry. As a result, none of us can be a happy person, our whole family will suffer, and then, eventually, society will be more troubled. So, it becomes clear that cultivating these kinds of basic spiritual values becomes crucial.

If you understand spiritual practice in its true sense, then you can use all twenty-four hours of your day for your practice. True spirituality is a mental attitude that you can practise at any time.

ngaging in training or a method of bringing about inner discipline within one's mind is the essence of a religious life, an inner discipline that has the purpose of cultivating these positive mental states. Thus, whether one leads a spiritual life depends on whether one has been successful in bringing about that disciplined, tamed state of mind and translating that state of mind into one's daily actions.

*Investigators have found that even an artifi-
cially induced frown or smile tends to induce
the corresponding emotions of anger or
happiness; this suggests that just 'going
through the motions' and repeatedly engaging in a positive behaviour can eventually
bring about genuine internal change.*—H.C.

Although one's experiences are a consequence of one's past deeds, that does not mean that the individual has no choice or that there is no room for initiative to change… One should not become passive and try to excuse oneself from having to take personal initiative on the grounds that everything is a result of Karma, because if one understands the concept of Karma properly, one will understand that Karma means 'action'… So what type of future will come about, to a large extent, lies within our own hands in the present. It will be determined by the kind of initiatives that we take now.

Now the secret to my own happiness, my own good future, is within my own hands. I must not miss that opportunity!